death songs

Robin Wyatt Dunn

TRANSCENDENT ZERO PRESS
HOUSTON, TEXAS

ISBN-13: 978-1-946460-26-4
Library of Congress Control Number: 2020939828

Printed in the United States of America

Transcendent Zero Press
16429 El Camino Real Apt. #7
Houston, TX 77062

FIRST EDITION

death songs

Robin Wyatt Dunn

Introductory note from the poet

they're saying it isn't poetry if I write about myself
that these words are hate

Thank you for coming. Although death unites all of us, we are each
free to meet him on our own terms. My own relationship with death
is as secret admirer, sometime suitor, and perhaps agitator: I want
him to come out and dance.

Come see the obscenities!
Endure the long night!
See the Reptile!

Don't be afraid. They're only words. These things that move our
limbs: engines of a kind. You can climb in, and rev it up with me,
and watch the terror fill the windshield. It's our right, as apes, to see
just what it is the sky can do, and these trees, before they both
collapse.

Many of these poems I wrote in Canada, so there's some of that cold
energy in here. And some of the combatant spirit here was stirred on
by me being an American there, and seeing what we're still fighting
about. This Revolutionary War that is never really over.

If Bergman can play chess with Death, I can at least sing him a lay or
two, before he gets me.

###

tear right and run the nil
all my pills and pillboxes show glowy manes and winters
solemn as rain
stark naked imperial power
stove ahead and shake the burial of the sky
imbue the wrought iron with your face

no never far away
just a kind of meditation on your death
the lesser of two bereaved is always in your bed
black putrefying greed
in the morning eggs
and in the car on the way to work
in the dungeon where you scrape and serve
where you
--what is it?--
where you were before it happened

was it a kind of war
stuck in your head?

--no, not that--

just a release.
like men from slavery
or me from your face

not long a wait
not stuck at dawn under your sheets
not meditating on the grave grief who sticks his claws into the
breaks
to mumble something splendid with relief
too much to wash over me:

not ready yet inside the breach:

the locked and loaded love affair of each to each
starving underneath the artist's eye upon the beach
bright and naked

drunk on the sound of the bass
its lace exciting all the things I couldn't say
like shamble jack
I didn't say that
or jimble thumb
and all the beginnings and runnings of the land
like batteries runneling beneath the level of the sin

no mistakes here:

only weapons for a war I don't know how to fight
ancient future weapons
locked in light and tied tight to the beat
sent to your heart and mine

get me the thang and angles in
the din exacts the land and pulls it back and in
to charge the awesome strumming of its retarded get the
mouth on fin
a fish man
he's a fish man
Dagon's jacking in to wave at Samson through the slight and
silver stim
cutting notes into the rubber
cutting notes into the leather
cutting notes into the stark and black
cutting notes into the facts as they exist
jacking up and down over the land
run right in place
I'll hold your hand to stand the weight
no fall from grace could be as sweet

god get out
right on track
any minute

the spirit of a nation is more than a story
it's a feeling in the air:
the way the birds move and the way the houses stand upon
the street
a relentless energy or heartbeat
underneath visible sight.

so we can copy nations
transpose buildings, cars, shops & stones
but the place and people shake over it the pall
of its nature:
sprite sound and word unutterable

level the city
reprogram the citizens
dig out the river
let the girl onto the raft

scratch the name
and dig into my flesh
the relish of the uterus and argonaut splendor is
I have the burrower in me
ten thousand names unseen
cut into my skin

garrulous genders
The Canadians!
Cut in their jumper.
righteous mad, but not enough yet.

which is it, eh?

Cake, cake, cake

The splendorous cake
Stuck on your thumb

Lick it off and tell me its name

Name the nation of your undoing

gemstones in the udder
burning terrible pouring over the biscuit
in my mouth

in my mouth

here is the guitar
behind the artillery

Here is Third Manassus
Crossing Lake Superior

Here is Pink Floyd

Overhead, the drones

Plant the flag over the battalion headquarters
Our battalion is a five year old girl
Dressed in the regalia of the revolution

Her face a mask of black

Inside her hand
The scroll of the poem

Inside the elementary school
we are painting pictures of the great battle

Second Hastings

The light heat
Stuck in the head
The white heat
prepping the mouth

My sound is the hills
struck by lightning
ushered under the wrapping fire
the name of the lightning is my mother
Her mouth is kissing the house
Before the word

if I name it it will flee
so I will not name it
no one must name it
not in a language of this Earth

(there is another Earth beneath this one
like this one
with a different colored sky)

perhaps I have named it already
and will be damned for it . . .

let us pretend I never named it
and that it can't be named
that no one will ever name it
neither in this language
or any other

let us pretend I am up against it
awake, rather than dreaming
alive,
not dead

let us pretend I have the rain on my shoulders from its ice
and that the sound of its earth is shaking over your feet
in waves

let us pretend you are already there
inside your feet
under the steps of the sky
your voice is spreading out over the firmament
lightning bulbs
on the estuarial feet of the stalags there

I know the name but cannot say it
because the place changes when the name is uttered

the sounds are still there, in my sleep

shaking against my skull
like the waters of the Nile

No, if I should wonder all the rest of it tonight I'd die.
Best to go to sleep,
And let the poem dream.

turning on
we are at 500 megahertz
2 klicks south of the hole

you told me you had the pie ready
I bought you roses
the sky is a color I have never seen
and the hole is like God
belching water

tuck me under the fall

one rage against the night tormented
one mark against the rage and rock
one talks to keep the beast at bay but
all is stopped
the ray of light,
the names and faces cut from wax are melting . . .

but the deeper one goes,
the truer are the names
stuck sure to the side of your arm
the armaments of nations
the rivers of the tombs
and the stark naked arches of the womb

guard my eyes the sky
and skirt the mangy wraith of my surprise
no one shall know otherwise

no one shall say which cruel intent is mine
the maker and the rice
the lover and the leerer
ready for the name

whose is it anyway
the beech and burst of wishes
thrust under the porch
to mate with whores

whose wraith am I
planted under the breeze

You'll know I'm coming when I raise my hand
Around the bend in the road
I'll raise up my hand
Under my time you've been so nearby
So glad and bright and close
Looking with me at the stars.

You'll know I'm coming when I raise up my hand,
To wave goodbye.

bring me death
in his bright eyes
I need to see his path over the sighs of the children and the
rafts of the sky

which mirror are the oceans
and who made it so?
I must deliver my hands into the dirt pile
to look for my soldier

boner boney bone
dig the raygun throne
shucking and jiving
jiving in the ten night hat
jiving to beat the man
who made me hate
eskate the circlet
and land this map
right over your porch
no shortage
no reportage
only the ten mile sand
and your worthless stare
we'll buy it any time

stare, and be heard
the block tight at the neck
and the strike in the mouth
each arch in a way
and each man
barbering the night helmet
enraged arranged at nines
earfuls and earfuls and earfuls

my tenderness

the wrought and wright
endeared
the rake and wrench embittered
stuck on the lonely claw
lizardly
storm auburn
name the children of the sea metal

stamped hammered into place
unredeemable
issued only once

dandelion drink
dark and natured stinky drink
stammering the religious think
of mine

down inside my heady think
dangerous and ready for the right
I hold onto my head
and watch the sky
he's like me
dying

give me your opponent slaughtered in the green
and give me all his things
give me his wife and jewelry
give me his name
I'll take it and I'll honor his house by burning it into the
ground

take my hand into the dark delight
all my heart
I have a secret for you
what I saw inside the light

some courier gave me the hand
benighted

I'm sorry but I had it in my mind to see you die.
All of my life I've seen it shining my mind
No gladder thing could be said
Than to see you dead inside the ground of my heart.

what have you got
show it to me

I'm counting it out
I heard you had it made

Now you may not have heard my name
But I've been coming into town to listen
to just what you think.

bright starling
summering the light
my dear dead starling summering the midnight light

black and white
red is the opposite of white
black is the opposite of night

tell me which star
tell me which deadly sky I'm in

tell me my heart
which bright deliverer I'm in
stuck on the moonlight ride
into destruction

burial rite
bid my wife raise my corpse into the sky

each bird who flies inside the dark
promises the end of your city

Hi hi hi ho

now I can hear the faint of heart
now I hear the grumbling
the alarm is going off
and people are shuffling their feet

they're suggesting that I've lost my mind
that I should shut up.

the telephone is playing a song
and I'm going to sleep

they're saying it isn't poetry if I write about myself
that these words are hate

now on my right
the drums

the black light underneath my ribcage
locked on love
never under any recompensation
or any kind of livery
all my friends have sighted the near part of the shit
bent into the dead night

this corpse
so beautiful
enriches my bow

whoever should grieve with my mouth
unaging
imbued with a knife inside
shining out of their eyes

let me kiss your lips
and give you the detonator

what rigor
curled under your husband
and your child
stemming light narrow and direct
along the ream and rowman
stamped dangerous into the names of the night
each one staring
each one buried like time inside of the size of the deep

what light keep
ready not too soon
for the starmount and ides
enclasped like a blanket in the child's arms

tear down the structure of the world
so that I might lie beside you
bent under the dream of the metal sky
no shelter but your hair
no words but the night

no never ever
never ever never
not or not
and not today
not every when I say
the mark and dark you took from me
inside this lightless place
I have a feeling how it's getting out:

streaming in your eyes
the shape of my upreaching earpiece:
taking hold to practice magic in the spaces in between your
toes
and over the surface of your skin:

never winter comes again under my life
never straight or rain or white
each black cause and right subsists inside the dream
I made of you
like licking sides of glass against the mucus

Bear the bridge and tie the mark
Listen to the music under the dark inside
Remember which parts were important.

The weeping inside the brain
The feeling that you were young.
The notion--however interdependent--
That it was yours in particular.

This atomization, not some evil thing from the government,
Just a figuration of your body against the dark
Tapping your fingers against your skull
And against the dashboard of your car.

I have you inside of me:
The locked lark and light of the region I knew then,
Buried inside the park underneath the strange lights of
California.

the dead night drinks my loneliness away
waiting outside for day
and each hour drinks too
the sky summoning up the strength to bring the bottle to its
lips:

remembering eternity

the crows are fighting over who has the longest memory
and I'm watching them
like a child watching the surf
wondering when he'll learn how to go inside

steer me close to the dawn
but not inside it
I want to see the light shake through the sight
rip slow the storm of my weary expenditure
towards its sky shrines

near enough
to lip the red edge of its cause and shine
like death dips under the drought to find the day:

all rusted dark inside
a distant melody heard on the submarine recording:
near so close

however narrow the gap
to desire
her knees will clap
electric sunbeam rapping against the door:

which raucous fluid
bright endearing the spark
shadowed and corked

spears the name of the mark
to find the day inside the dun

which runt hand
tabling the armaments of the main band
fierce and sallow by the reason
uttered only alone

the names of desire
run slow beneath the continents
whipping up
to fill the gap

They tell me that I'm done
run under,
a dun colored Dunn
scrubbed clean:

They say I'm a bully
with my words,
Unclean.

They say I hate the right parties,
And love the wrong,
That I put the wrong things in,
And leave the right ones out.
Like some strange cake,
Inedible.

They say I shouldn't say it
Be silent,
we know better;
you have the wrong color on your skin,
and the wrong shape between your legs,
Too old or young,
Not ready,
Too ready,
The piston in the mix not firing,
& Firing too hard

Fire hard at me
I've readied my chest for your blow
I'll take the bullet in and grow it into my second castle
Lead and steel and rock
And I'll keep your head inside it.

dare me under sun
naked running
to you

drunk me the wretched answer to the gun
stumbling through the digits of your name
too many names
but I keep counting--

drive me closer
to kiss the swollen surface of the water

Nero takes the violin and tests the bow
Inside the sparks are grown
Charred skin and hands

The ruins of the night
The raged dying against the light
Rage and rage
Inside the abattoir of day
Rage and rage inside the quiet

Name for me the poem Nero wrote
over the households
over the marked hands

The black copses throw themselves into the air

Dear dead heart
The rest is easy
Rain and meant mead
Married beneath the sun-stained trees
Never doubt my love
Though it comes confining shouts
and crazy talk
I have the bones
for you

your holiness
the empire spike
empiric delayed light
filling the galley of our thoughts like rain
empyrean design
stark adder
naked knife
thrusting up from the soil to reign the sky

my mother never sees its wimpled heights
the way it blasts the blue light out over the sea and city

mock grace

lyrical god of steel and stone
hermaphroditic
changing

thrust over the night to roar

my orthodox delight
my obelisk

a well well well
a well well well
a well well well
a well well well
a well well well

my heart

Never fear what I think
I am already dead;
A ghost to you.
The reparations for eternity
Are not so deep;
we can have them here at tea
To shatter your dreams.

No one else shall surmise
How sweet it is
to see you come over to the trees
And drink the water of the nightless night
where I've been keeping my hands close to the bark
watching the sky.

I shall rupture your temple
with my whim
Samson Agonistes in my jimjams
Punning in:

The fray is mine
so kneel
and deliver me your word that you have seen my face
sunning sunlight dimpled in the dark delight

Sharpen the knife and hold the gun inside your brain
Johnny Mnemonic in memes:

whet the edge and curl the fence around your dreams:
each one in position
shield overhead
and feet in the dirt

the beam of nature hurts to wield
like the finger in the paint
and the mind around the whip

each man extends his arm to win the day
detonating the sound of rain

drunk faddle
fiddle mad and mixed within to take off pants
and lick my tits
like luscious lips of raspberry bliss
no better than anywhere
not ready for anything
not supposed to do anything
and not knowing
how to feel

love my energy and drink it in
for I've been feeling just how to reel you in
like cheese
on the numbered list
like lovers on their secret tryst
exist for me inside the mirrored avenue
of the rent stake
and live five
ready to die:

deal me in
I'm ready to play
with my tongue

on the mark
get set

open your mouth

and tell me everything

all of my dear love
shaking around the room
naked on the cross
buried under the road
shackled and screaming
all of my alma maters
each one luminous and armed
terrible and darkbright shades of the moon
scattering over the sky in pieces

each one of them beautiful
glistening with light
pieces of your soul
sucked down into your body
to dance like a blender
overflowing with smoothie
splattering the kitchen with pink

Come see the obscenities!
Endure the long night!
See the Reptile!

soft,
desperate one
your feet are steady
and your hands lithe
there are the doors in blue
and the red knife
everything we could have wished
and not better

each sound in the gull flap
the rotor throat
and the pleasure of women
carried in the night
out and over the mountains
where I am dreaming

we could do everything that you wanted
burn the church and spread the ash
cut the king and marry the wax
string the knife and chant the frame at night
each living soul to carry all the merry lights
across your neck:

we could do everything you liked
like a stone into the lake
and with closed eyes
admit
that you're not quite ready yet
to rule

turn me dead
and burn my heart again
and burn it black
burn my skin so I can take the mainframe
out and in
and out again
like Death himself

tear off my head and carry it on the subway
so I can watch your face from your purse

and though I be Orpheus
and you be a Maenad
and you abstain from liquor
and I from the lyre

still I will sing headless
in death
to you

it burns but that's all right
I've gotten used to hell
and all its shapes

the pyre of the night is bright and wide
and I've seen you there
hovering over my grave

I want to write you someone beautiful
if the Atlantic were a person
if the pina colada
and the 5 year vacation
were a man

I want to make you merrier
washed brunt and bare
next to my cock
for the duration
under the bridge
under the edge of my hair

Nereid non-pareil
devil eye and mad
like me
buried deep
under the nation
buried deep under the nation in the air

hatchet my prose
and take a piece to eat
I don't know anything
I only grow it for you to eat

nations
gift givers
barred hands
narrow agents
stand and delight
beautiful
locked men and chains!
cut them open on the floor
and give me god

name takers and oarsmen
shapes and sifter sands
stake and ready men
women under the broad trireme of sky
daggers and dead legacies
kept under the weight of the hull
under my hull the rake and rill of the wasp and sea
shall fill me and mine for you,
dear dread heart
to time the way and say how I have come to thee
not free but shredded and serene
to see how far it is to the edge of the land

jangling courses stop and sigh
over my pleasing face
jutting slow beneath the band of slaves
who pierce the rock and bend the mountain to name our
callow and enduring brace
clattering and scraping
with bright eyes

shave and start the music

oh dear dark heart
don't despair
the mighty meat she isn't there
never ready for your airs
or wreaths of hair
not susceptible to your largesse
not here
not alive
and not so beautiful as you insist
my lovely
your serenade sputtered in your cheek
your cackle and your auburn claw
aren't ready quite yet

wheel the weight in behind
eye the eye
mark the marker
and shelter each incision from the line
(who hovers over everything)

love's a slow tap
trying to keep the necessary tact
between looking and going blind

we won't need everything
just a piece

we shouldn't care, not yet; we're not ready to care, for however close you may come we have methods in place and reasons, filed carefully, in black and white, love not yet, and not too soon, and never in its right place, not this hour, not this year. All the leashes we have left we are tightening down, ants over the carcass of the nation, Lilliputians over the great body, hips and curls, to secure the prize . . . but we little mean men and women, driven mad, locked in futile work and made naked under the storms and winters and exhaust of the century, no longer know how to make use of this body of desire: each hour, and each minute, starved of affection and reason, made into the tools of our masters like so many gaskets in the engine of despair, revving up, 60 rpm, 70, 80, 90, and now five thousand: to know just how it is, and what must be the shape of its nearness, sliced and delivered by the deli man luscious and paper-thin, sweet-scented and still just arduous enough, after each disaster winnowing its shape to peer through the hole in the wreckage and determine the right method of escape, and the quickest method of return, to your body:

the timing itself can bring us to it, nearing the ultimate decision, not of marriage or sex or reconciliation, divorce, argument or exile but merely ennui, thicker than butter, crammed over your face like a terrible helm, yet so necessary to its work, in the timing belt of love, to rear and regard the self with a modicum of wherewithal, to know just what is it, and where we are, and what kind of thing is happening, over however great a distance, we keep love alive in the imagination — perhaps it is born there as well — and locked tight in the body, a slug in the gut, shocked and shaken deep under the folds of your skin and the limpid leisure of your bones, majordomo of desire:

the leash, if slack, still holds us close in its embrace, to say, once again: *not yet* — not just yet, however desperate insane the shape of love has become, no matter how necessary or nearby, and no matter what shape it threatens to take. Not just yet, though it be true and honest and even serene, because to move too soon would be to break this shell and spell of despair, like the ice combs over Superman's livid corpse, and the bonds over Gulliver's body, riotous and new, raging against the meaningless enforcement of laws which cannot even be read, and though its exigencies are written into the body in blood and ash and fire and salt all of its presences in their delivery mark the soul with its righteous energy, to recreate the spell of your doom and dark denial and then release the body, hunter over the wood, to the armaments and dreams of your every desire:

this is not a play
although you could say I am wearing a costume
I could lead men in the army

but who are we fighting?

let us say that I am a real man
with manly habits
and let us say that the reason I have come to stay is that I must
destroy you

It's nothing personal, you understand.
It's just something that needs to be done.

First I must let the coffee steep.
Then I must toast my bagel and spread cream cheese on it.
And then I must destroy you.

this play--which is not a play!--is well produced
and the lines are interesting.
even the lighting is well considered.

when I arrive on stage,
I will be carrying a gun
and a small scroll

perhaps it is an announcement
or a death warrant

I will write your name onto it
either onto the scroll, or onto the gun (they're the same thing)
and then we can get down to business.

now and better
almighty pants and sometimes a shave
the belly coming out a bit
and the moon
the ride of your wife
the light of the loon inside
folded under the case in the trunk

a machine gun?
a case of beer?
presents for the kids

the careful dodge of questions
the nearness of the dawn
like the nearness of destruction
the closest friend
light on your cheek:

just a fuck
a fall to bliss
and perdition it insists
all the leashes and the ties
subsist on these enticing lies
writ into the starving sundry burials of your body

jade and black are keeping me awake
it's the dead hour charming tracts of deepest blood red
the multitudinous seas
in light (of the mind):

I have this feeling in the knees
or somewhere in the spine
this lightness of the rising electric

walt whitman,
or one of his many homunculi,
is tapping on the window of my skin
wanting in to speak:

rumble rumble rumble
rumble tumble melon fine and dandy
shock full of brandy
shocked full of light inside my dark apartment

the pendant heart is wicked
a lover married to the hour
bent in love's hate
a creature made of brine
salt stark and tall

stark and naked

the beating heart is wicked
in its waiting
naked shafts and shifting purposes
beneath and over the brain

the braking heart is naked
stopping short of the stuff
short of the cuff it's gruff
to use perusing each in turn
the ought and axe and weight
who grinds the lover's asps into a painful soup:
agitated washing
frothing soap

dear and stunted burial man
runty carriage-hand
lurker and drab
eager to know
how the bitter love of the air
negated but even in winter, sweet
the nary lure of the evil
charming and ready
like a leer from the woman of the house
who has you in her keeping
starmy and swarmy
kept so neat
the bark of the bill
and the bread of the brange
like love,
it makes the stew clench
its meaning

my burial man
broad-handed and lithe
like a hunted oak
curled under the raptor
nurtured by the dainty ties
of the winter-moist air

he stands with his ax in his hand

what do you want me to do with it
the just and hate
the naked date with love
in his hideous forms?

how is it that the names insist
how which is right
and which isn't quite
and which should be before
and which left behind

tell me how it is that you decided
just what it was to say
and what it was to mark the saying
to bring out the briny world
slipping from your pearly hand
into the dark under of your will

stormcropper in your breezy arms
charm and staid
lock and load the rounds of your heart
each in his turn
for all the bright beneath your eyes
and ours

let out the shark to jump into the light
each hour and each night
to growl and to laugh
to show us how grand it can be

in your leprosy, my friend
we know your name
and if you lose a limb you'll gain a hand in ours

every minute to the punch

punch it in and we'll see if the computer can add it up
and if not
we'll just greet the band naked
to show it how it stands between the world and the land
each peasant to his ghost

and each lord under the gun

tell me how it is again
I want to listen all night

the leash is on your neck
my countrymen
my ladies fair
wenches in the lock
women on the droves
watching their hands
for sign of error

naked spire in the field!
black hour and weed loft!
storm and glad repast and wise!

take heed,
the meat is the doing
cut close to the bone

for Vatsala Radhakeesoon

in the stands and in the stead
with your daily bread and height
to stand and bake the night out of the land
unlovely wrath

on the arms and in the head
the meer and make-do catch up in your lap
to bright the stars with your laugh

we can hear it
when you stand

naked boy and thunder's broad hand
son of my bed
shire and fair gnarr
gnawing the groan
to know the minute
to know the hand

son of the mine and of the sky
son of blood and stones in the back
stones in the back of the chance

hearken if you can
to the leash in the sky
who vibrates under your tongue
his kind ensues in yours
if you listen
if you speak the sounds we need

it can be any good sound
a rock on a stump
or your hands on your hands
the tree on your foot
or the dirt on your house
and the air in the flue

thundering

boy of the land
I have you in my mind
I want you to lead us to war

inside your mind
are rubber bands
I'd fire one if I can
if you'll tell me where to shoot

poets and pickle-eaters
craw-chains and shakers of mettle
stickle pains and cacklers
in their deep mane
law for me
under your hat and ways
inside your hands and days
the long arm of the line

eave of my childhood
tarmac and mud
elm and tarpaper bus stop
Houston apartment
wyoming sun
running in the thunder

I command you
on your pledge
to come
and wage war

bring me ten men like that one
burning all the night
bar the sky and send in the threats to time
the fever in the mud

fray the air and scale the castle wall
with your song around

take me close to your chest
so I can listen to your heart

Lo and behold!
Leer, and bake.
It's come so far, but not enough.
Throw the bread into your enemy's face,
To see how he wears it.

Does he carry it under his sleeve?
Inside of his pants?
Do his balls drop below his knees?

where does his hair go,
And where is it situated
And are you ready to take him?

Lay and be set
in the name of the river
ball out your loaded steps
and be reticent before the shape of the rain
for it is speaking to you threats
and the names of the children of your attackers
bred under your lamps
like yours
to stare wildly into your face

the thaw is like a slow blimp
lifting us above the ground
the rain now drives away the dreams of the ground
and gives us instead the trees'
ratcheting over the sky the shape of their plans

The purple Lightning is beautiful
To Delight the eye of the child
A naked melancholy ship
Wintered in warmth

buried under the gift
light and burning
we'll wade till the pound is right
shut down over legs and hands
the cliff of the limb and bright
changing over your head

dies drear and deadly deranged
deal me in

marry me to the sprit and central shock
to mar my middling man inside
he needs the launch
the mask and scrape against the bark

run dun
and me

each picture
scuffed over the ruin of the land
quakes my agony inside
to par and paint the open veil of your life
waking scarified and white

the Jews are holding a sign
saying "kill them all"
for their proud festival
waving their colors over the boulevard

the blood runs down their neck
quiet and graceful
staining the cement

each one of their faces is stupid
locked in the expression of the god
who wants their flesh

what is the idea of it?

to pitch you into the dark.

shut you tight inside and make you scrape against the walls
with your hands
to make you see the light inside

to brutalize you in the street so you can't speak
can't say the thing you need

to deny you which flavor and which man inside your hand
was yours
that man yourself

the idea of falling in love
the idea of the fist

come to Canada to forget
all your many troubles in the alleys of the trees
and the neighbors' stares

there's no sweeter than sound than misery in Canada
the blackest sight over the sweet

come to Canada to forget your head
forget your dreams

He's on a bender in his bed
dreaming of what was spent
dreaming of the life he led
in Spain
or some other hotter country

it doesn't matter
all roads lead to Canada to die

brushed from the scar of the land
taken into your hand
and white

come to Canada and you'll forget
the name you had inside your head
there is no other now to die
just the one you might encounter in the dark
who prays in sleep
his desires are the fright
and the manacles of midnight staring wide into the dark

we have it all in Canada
bright and white
nameless and obscene we shuffle dark on light
into the faces of the people that we knew

tell me the name of your fed
the name of your dead
the names of your lonely wear
and the name of your sticks

tell me the name of your kitchen
and the name of your chamber pot
the name of your hallway lamp
the name of your door
and the porch in front

tell me the name of your road
and the name of your hand

in the name of your hand
in the name of your hand

behold this place
and make it your own

Dear heart
Rancorous and sally shrank
built dead and draghted weight
not expiring on the day
not ready for the time
turbulent arm
spreading the glee over the mark
shrouded shark
beckoning the dark
my love

Beat the air with your praise
Beat the mainstay with your hair
Arm the recompense with your cheer
Leaden and near
Like the meat of the year
Stinky and sweet
Black with rage and marriage
Enough underneath
The pitiful skin
To darn the mean and meaning of these spent
Like your youth

Blast the pain and cure the neck
Shred the contract and secure the Triple Sec
For Margarita is coming down the stairs with her Mini gun
The Terminator tattooed on her arm

we can do it
though the riveters may be dead
and the ships are sunk
though the flag's a lie
and the country too

the bare and broad exactitude
of love
invites the pain to see
its legions

ripped up from the earth
cut into shape
for the using well

The People, Yes
and then, the People, No

and then
The People, Yes

marked into grief
for the killing
and the songs that heal it

what kind of reckoning is it
what is the moral accounting system:
an abacus
or a scar on your cheek;
notches in the bedpost
and on your hips

what kind of melancholy is it
who seizes your wrists
and slams them into the car door
ratcheting up the sky over your head
for the show

Protect me, god of the Woods,
From my sadness,
And use the shade in your bark
To circuit my spirit,
In darkening rounds,
Over the earth.

In the black hounds,
Feed me my mushrooms,
To dine under the stars,
And give me hours of steep quiet,
Shaking against my head
Wind on the mast of my neck.

I'll kill for you;
If you need it;
Though I am only a stupid man.

Give me peace to see the light,
Who murders the silence of your surround,
With its pinioned hands.

burn with my delight
over the furniture in fright
tie tight the stems inside your dress
and bend to tarnish all the stresses and regrets
you carried all this way:

a legionnaire's commission
stuck up in your bum

and on its way out:

in renouncing the nation
and your writ

we'll slit open the letter of your will
we'll set it aflame
to find its patient nurturing circle-fire
cumming around the edge of the noxious waste of the past
licking the edges of the burning husk of your apartment

care for me under the river dead
not alive but dead
sanctified in the flood

sharpen my casket in the deafening numb
break open the fever of my thumb
the blood

the blood is dandy
the blood shares the narrow channel of the pirouette beneath
the server-mask
of the basin
swimming round the continent
and continents

light me wet and reeking
wreaking lava in my mouth

lay me down beneath the waves
so I may serve the barrier reef in black
so I might carve my name into your dreams when you're
asleep
atop the walls and steep crevasses of your needs

each one infinite and white
Dover beneath the sea
glimmering

If I should die before I break
The season of regret
I pray the cord my baggage take
miles deep inside the prison lights of my mind

deeper than I've ever been

where guards name the rights
of my hands

if I should die before I stake
the light

before I take the night away
before I bake the tomb inside my dreams:

then deliver me

naked

name me and deliver me

into your horror show and hour
into your steaming pile of shit

the nameless feeling of the slit-curse
the theater of the nation state
the theater of the prayer

East Pacific Theater

B2 engines sharking the night air
take me inside them to season the nature spirit
and nurturing friend
of the blood

we'll bury you all night
each sequined dress
each strand of hair
we'll name your every prayer
your last grace

we'll bury you and entomb your thoughts and your deck of
cards
your church nursery farewell

each heap of earth
each heartbreak
each bloody symphony cut into the wax of your dreams
I'll play them all
and sing

take me with you in the night air
some Gulf Stream Florida beach
Black and nameless and free

give me the taste of your tongue before you sleep
so I can watch you swim away

bury me and bleed
the dark and ebony farewell
need the bark and bread
of your sleet stained trees

need the naked spurn of your greed
lantern eyes
and twittering hands

board me
a teenager in some Black Market Eton
I'll carry the knife
and I'll carry your toes
into the liquid fire of the black lake

just give me the diamond
of your message
just gasp me your secret

I only want to know how far you made it down within

now I know the trees again
their hooded faces slumbering
the possession of the world

inside my California credit card of memories
(almost, but not quite maxed out)

tell me the reason that you slept through the night
while I was awake

and tell me why you couldn't see what happened

I know it anyway

for the God's frightening face
needs no poetry or disgrace

his eyes are portals in the leaves
trembling fire for the signal from Troy
ten thousand mountains deep

one by one from Pergamum to Keratea

my name on your breath

give me one more minute
to record the sound of your feet
tapping on the window sill in the street

a San Francisco treat
not Rice a Roni

but one of those old 1960s apocalypses
where Jack Kerouac is bleeding out in your Buick

and all you can do is laugh

the stony sound of the leftover people
kicks into gear outside the apartment complex
bad luck feet

the sound of the river is inseparable from its ghost
a dead monarch still trying to breathe

the light of the tribe is weight
shuffling down through the gaps in the trees

the nature of the camp is free
for just one day

how long will the day last?
these thousand years
the length of English

broken over the steps
it's meat

a pony getting so old you can see its bones
but its eyes are greedy and black
and needing sleep

there are no nations in our feet
we just keep moving them over the same tracks
to see if we still need to see

what ghost cuts me
myself
shuts me in the door of the light

turns me in to the demon that I am
small god and wight

white chieftain of the broken bones
carols stuck on the megaphone
chanting extremities

the bark of my skin
changing under the sky to see
who I am now

what demon is it who chants the curtain
of the darkening day
cut into my skin

POSTSCRIPT

I'm a crazy person these days—though it all depends on where you stand. My position is that Covid-19 does not exist—that it is part of a long-term scheme by men and women with too much power to control the human population. The response, of course, is very real. And that is really what has been affecting everyone. This house arrest. This new authoritarian presence on the street and in the shops. The same as the old authoritarian presence, just several times larger.

Authority is funny—from the same root as author, naturally—meaning grower. Those who grow have a natural authority. And the ruling class is growing us, on their human ranch. And this is a new Enclosure Act.

Take to the hills, I say. And arm yourselves—with words and guns.

- -

This is one in a long series of crises, originating perhaps in the early 17th Century. This is in many ways a continuation of the Thirty Years War, where noblemen from all over Europe colluded to slaughter peasants in untold numbers.

It is not politic to say it, but messianic Judaism—the belief that the Chosen People ought to rule the world, with the advent of their Messiah—also was born in that century. And it has plagued us for 400 years now. The Bank of England, and later the Federal Reserve, are both products of the Babylonian system, via the Talmud.

Anyone who brings up these awkward facts is labeled a Jew-hater these days—and these Messianic Jews, like Jared Kushner, Trump's son-in-law, attempt to destroy their careers. Being a Jew is no defense in this regard—Norman Finkelstein and Gilad Atzmon have also been black-balled.

As for me, I found myself ejected from the nation of Canada for pointing out that the *New York Times* is a Zionist paper. These are the times we have come to.

I don't know what our 'masters' are planning to do now that they have everyone holed up, waiting for their death blows . . . or so they think. But I do know it's an odd situation to be in, where friends, family and peers attack everyone who bothers to point out the truth—that this has all happened before, and Messianic, Talmudic Judaism, with its core beliefs of racial supremacy ordained by a Father Creator, are at the root of many of them.

Until more people are willing to address this uncomfortable fact, we will continue to huddle in our caves, wondering what has happened to us.

Acknowledgements

"nations" and "name takers and oarsmen" first appeared in A New Ulster #81, June 30 2019.

"We shouldn't care" first appeared in Riverbabble #35, Bloomsday issue, July 3, 2019.

"poets and pickle-eaters" first appeared in Harbinger Asylum, July 14, 2019.

"what ghost cuts me" first appeared at The Piker Press, October 21, 2019.

"what kind of reckoning is it" first appeared at The Piker Press, December 16, 2019.

"level the city" first appeared in Concrete Mist Press anthology, edited by Heath Brougher, February 29, 2020.

Robin Wyatt Dunn was born in Wyoming in 1979. The son of a geologist father and a potter mother, he has lived in six states, the U.K., and Canada. New Pop Lit called him "one of the most talented writers in America." He has been nominated for several awards, including the Rhysling, Elgin, Pushcart and Best of the Net. He was once a finalist for Poet Laureate of Los Angeles. Currently he lives in Tucson, Arizona.

More by Robin Wyatt Dunn

POETRY
Poems from the War
Science Fiction: a poem!
Sunsborne
Wine Country
What Black Delirious Daylight Sets You Forward in the Boat
Remarriages
Debudaderrah
Black Heart Uprising
Some Dredged Deep

NOVELS
Los Angeles, or American Pharaohs
My Name is Dee
Fighting Down into the Kingdom of Dreams
Line to Night Island
A Map of Kex's Face
Julia, Skydaughter
Conquistador of the Night Lands
White Man Book
Colonel Stierlitz
Black Dove
City, Psychonaut
2DEE
This Isn't One of the Stories I Remember
The Black King of Kalfour
Sitting on the Floor

SHORT STORIES
Dark is a Color of the Day

PLAYS
Last Freedom

FILMS
A Wilderness in Your Heart
Party Games
American Messenger

www.ingramcontent.com/pod-product-compliance
Lightning Source LLC
Chambersburg PA
CBHW071619040426
42452CB00009B/1390